A Bouquet of Hearts

Shayla Hill

BookLeaf Publishing

India | USA | UK

Presentation by *BookLeaf Publishing*

Web: www.bookleafpub.com

E-mail: info@bookleafpub.com

ISBN: 9789363306165

First edition 2024

To all the hearts that have allowed me in and the ones that poured love back into me. A reminder to my four: Dedriana, Aviana, Brieana and Shayne to continue to allow love to freely flow through you.

"Reflection of Myself"
A Sonnet

Looking at you I find a reason to smile
You lift the weights off my shoulders
Providing consolation not felt in a while
You bear the burden as gracefully as one of
Gods soldiers

You've been the main reason for my laughter
Through what seems to be my darkest hour
Coming in as the climax of this chapter
Strictly on a mission to empower

Your daily affirmations are the reason for my
strength
You've been my rock, I'm leaning on you
I'll go the distance with you no matter the length
My eyes meeting yours when I wake is my
favorite view

A reflection of myself so beautifully packaged
Handling my heart with care though it's already
damaged.

"Love Visits"
A Haiku

Such a short-lived love
Only here for a moment
Joy, peace and goodbye.

"Heartbroken"
An Acrostic Poem

Heaven couldn't wait for an Angel like you
Even though you were our provider and
protector here
Always caring for us with so much love
Really setting a standard on how we should be
treated
Thank you for taking on that responsibility.
Being biologically yours wouldn't have changed
a thing
Realistically speaking you were all that I knew
Otherwise, I'd be without a father at all.
Keeping memories of you tucked tightly in my
heart
Expecting no other heartbreak to hurt this bad
Never forgetting that I had the very best dad.

"Rearranging Love"
A Villanelle

Our forever isn't done, forever is just changing
A promise to love has been made, so
Our love hasn't ended, instead it's rearranging.

Smiles and laughter we've been exchanging
For so many years, so you should know
Our forever isn't done, forever is just changing.

Supporting each other, one thing that's
unchanging
Though a certain relationship we did outgrow
Our love hasn't ended, instead it's rearranging.

So much about us we're constantly arranging
But through us love does still flow
Our forever isn't done, forever is just changing.

The places we'll see, we're still ascertaining
The love in this world to our children we'll show
Our love hasn't ended, instead it's rearranging.

Your role in my life has been interchanging.
Filing each other with love until we overflow.
Our forever isn't done, forever is just changing.
Our love hasn't ended, instead it's rearranging.

"Slowest Heartbreak"
A Nonet

I've loved you from your very first breath.
Years have passed and the love has grown.
I still smile when I see you.
Let me take care of you.
I know you're growing.
Let me help you.
I love you.
Slow down.
Wait!

"Here You Are"
A Dansa

I've been searching and here you are
Looking everywhere and you've been right here
Someone to love and now it's clear
I didn't even have to go very far
I've been searching and here you are

I look in the mirror and there you appear
Its kind of crazy, but this love is premier
The sweetest thing, like a song played on a
guitar
I've been searching and here you are

I haven't given the love you deserve I fear
But all of that's changing starting this year
You deserve the best, you really are a star
I've been searching and here you are

This kind of love I can't let disappear
Without it I'm sure the damage will be severe
Loving myself despite every scar
I've been searching and here you are.

"Shayne"
A Tanka

All I want to do
Is protect you from this world
I pray I don't fail
I'll love you through all life's pains
Shayne you can still count on me.

"Daddy Would Be Proud"
A Pantoum

We can look back and laugh because
We've been through the struggle together
Somehow even the bad memories are ok
Look what we made it through

We've been through the struggle together
Look at how strong we've become
Look what we made it through
Let's celebrate our growth

Look at how strong we've become
With everything that could have broke us
Let's celebrate our growth
We deserve a moment to relax

With everything that could have broke us
Here we are still standing
We deserve a moment to relax
Look at us still pushing forward

Here we are still standing
And I'll never leave your side
Look at us pushing forward
Each little step such a big success

And I'll never leave your side
This is where I've been for as long as I can
remember
Each little step such a big success
And we'll always celebrate each other

This is where I've been for as long as I can
remember
Daddy would be smiling and so proud of us
And well always celebrate each other
So glad I can lean on you

Daddy would be smiling and so proud of us
Look at who we're becoming
So glad I can lean on you
We're so strong because we have one another.

"Good"
A Free Verse

Good mornings are only good when my eyes
meet yours
Otherwise, I could just go back to sleep.
Good mornings are only good when I wake up in
your arms
Hold me tight baby, I'm yours to keep.

Good days are only good when I talk to you
throughout
If I'm not talking to you, what's there to talk
about?
Good days are only good when I get to hear "I
love you"
Sometimes that's what is needed so I can push
through.

Good nights are only good when I get to kiss
your lips
Followed by your hands caressing me.
Good nights are only good when I end them with
you
When it comes to my happiness you hold the
key.

Good times are only good because you are here
My smile is not the same when you aren't near.
Good times are only good because you are the
best
If I'm giving the lesson you're passing every
test.

"Brieana"
A Cinquain

Brie Brie
Happy, Pretty
Laughing, Smiling, Giving
The sweetest, Gentlest thing I know
Beauty

"Aviana"
A Limerick

Aviana my love, such a wonderful surprise
Always ready to fight when problems arise
You'll always be my favorite assistant
When I need you, you're never resistant
Your sense of humor of however is the best
prize!

"Dedriana"
A Minute Poem

Dedriana, my first-born love
Gift from above
Helped me to grow
More than you know

You're always so understanding
Not demanding
A giving heart
Right from the start

Forgive me for all my defeats
And empty seats
I love you girl
And every curl.

"You"
A List Poem

You are everything to me
More than I could ever ask for
So glad I can say we
Its not just me anymore
I love when we kiss
I love how you touch me
I love talking to you
I love how you love me
I love your eyes
I love the way you look
I love your voice
I love when you cook
I love when you smile
I love how you talk
I love your body
I love how you walk
I love how you sound
I love how you moan
I love how you breathe
I love how you own
I love every bit of you
So don't you ever leave
I promise to stay here
Its your love I want to receive.

"The Past"
A Decima

A whirlwind love story gone wrong
Exciting but so dangerous
A love we no longer discus
We tried to make it last so long
Relationship wasn't that strong
I could say I love and hate you
And they would both be very true
We gave it all that we could give
A love that we did still outlive
I can say cause of you I grew.

"Christine"
A Tritina

I couldn't ask for a better mother
To guide me through this life
No one can love and care for me the way you do

If it wasn't for you I wouldn't know what to do
You taught me how to be a mother
And how to care for a life

Because of you I've lived a happy life
Finding joy in everything I do
You really are an amazing mother

I'll do anything for you, my mother and friend
for life.

"On You"
A Diminishing Verse

Let me sit in your lap like you're my chair
Running my hands through each strand of hair
I wanna be in your skin and breathe the same air

I can promise from you I'll never go astray
I'd be back at your door just like a stray
Just serve yourself to me on a tray

"Reminders"
An Alphabet Poem

Always be proud of yourself
Because you deserve it
Create love wherever you go
Don't let anyone stop you
Even if you happen to fall get up
Falling isn't failing
Go out and enjoy yourself
Happiness is around every corner
I love you
Just the way you are
Keep pushing forward
Love yourself with each step
Make sure to breathe, you've got this
Never give up on yourself
Open your heart for love
Peace, joy and happiness
Quiet your mind
Remember you can do this
Self love is important
Trust in your self
Under every circumstance
Victory is yours
With or without an audience
Xenial is how you are

You're the best you you can be
Zestful personality, carry it with you.

"Love"
An Epigram

Easy to receive
But difficult to give
If you don't experience love
Then how do you live?